Kanban Rem

Agile Lessons from Strategy Games

8 Essays on Comparing Kanban with StarCraft

KANBAN REMASTERED

Agile Lessons from Strategy Games

8 Essays on Comparing Kanban with StarCraft

Published by Clemens Lode Verlag e.K., Düsseldorf

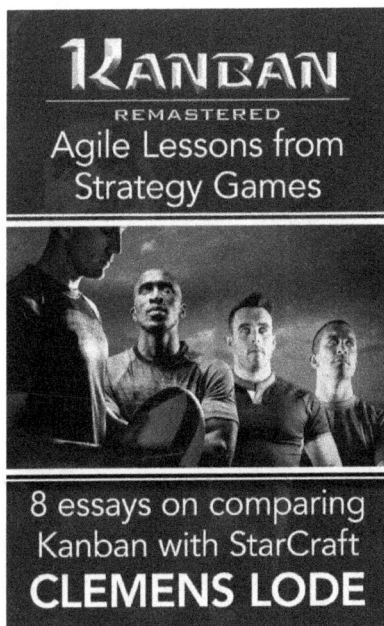

2019, Second Edition

ISBN 978-3-945586-66-2

Edited by: *Conna Craig*
Cover design: *Jessica Keatting Graphic Design*
Image sources: *Shutterstock, iStockphoto*
Icons made by http://www.freepik.com from
http://www.flaticon.com is licensed by CC 3.0 BY
(http://creativecommons.org/licenses/by/3.0/)
Subscribe to our newsletter. Simply write to newsletter@lode.de or
visit our website https://www.lode.de.

Printed on acid-free, unbleached paper. MANAGEMENT
PSYCHOLOGY

Introduction

神の一手—*Kami no Itte*—Japanese, roughly meaning "move of God" or "godly move"—describes an entirely new insight concerning a move during the game called "Go." Such a move is a goal taught to students to be more attentive toward less obvious maneuvers, leading the students to focus on alternatives. Likewise in management, first put aside the conspicuous answers (like adding more people to an already late project) to make way for an objective mind and attention to alternatives. In management, the challenge is to discover the potential of the team and your organization and to build upon that.

THIS BOOK SHOWS some of the 神の一手—*Kami no Itte*—of management, focused on the Kanban methodology and the computer game StarCraft. *Kanban Remastered* provides ideas for a Kanban coach to teach a team about Agile principles by building upon the team members' knowledge of games like StarCraft.

Contents

Publisher's Note

Thank you for keeping up the tradition of reading books. You and your fellow readers have created a market for this book. I hope that I can meet your expectations and I am looking forward to feedback from your side, no matter whether it is positive or negative. To send general feedback, mention the book title in the subject of your message and simply send it to feedback@lode.de. You can also contact us at https://www.lode.de/contact if you are having a problem with any aspect of the book, and we will do our best to address it. Also, we cordially invite you to join our network at https://www.lode.de.

Although I have taken every care to ensure the accuracy of the content, mistakes do happen. If you find an error in one of my books, I would be grateful if you would report this to me. By doing so, you can help me to improve subsequent versions of this book and maybe save future readers from frustration. If you find any errata, please report them by visiting https://www.lode.de/errata, selecting the book title, and entering the details. Once verified, the errata will be uploaded to our website. You will, of course, be credited if you wish.

Best regards,

Clemens Lode
CEO, Lode Publishing
Düsseldorf, Germany, July 1st, 2019

Preface

It HAS BEEN 20 YEARS since the release of StarCraft, with a "remastered" version coming out this summer (2017). Having been an avid player, I only now realize that a surprising amount of what we know as "Agile project management" is actually implicitly part of a regular game of StarCraft.

Being an Agile coach, I realized that especially in industries with teams with a gaming background, coaching lessons might benefit if I could show the relationship between games and Agile methodology. I was able to explain management methodology in a language that the tech-savvy audience understands.

StarCraft, the most popular real-time strategy game of all time, is all about producing and deploying as many game units as possible at just the right time. This book is about the relationship between StarCraft and Kanban. When your team knows StarCraft but not Kanban, this book will provide you with a series of analogies to allow a better and easier understanding of Agile principles. It is written in a light-hearted tone, similar to how you might chat with a fellow coach about your Agile experiences implementing Kanban, taking for granted that you have experience with StarCraft.

Despite the subject of my previous book, *Scrum Your Jira!* and despite Scrum being the most popular Agile methodology (at least on paper), I decided to compare StarCraft with *Kanban* instead. The reason is that StarCraft knows no separate roles, planning phases, or sprints and is all about managing your limited time to give commands on the battlefield.

Currently, Kanban is one of the most popular Agile management techniques besides Scrum and has also found its way away from pure logistics to software development. It can be used in other industries or work fields, but most of the examples I will bring up will be about software.

Ultimately, though, my personal stake in this subject is my interest in how the world works. Twenty years ago, I had a dream: to learn from nature. Reading about evolutionary algorithms that solved complex problems, step by step, fascinated me. It was the reason why I got into computers, and it was the reason I later embraced Agile development principles. During my computer science studies, I combined this interest with my hobby of playing StarCraft, which is why I chose StarCraft as an example to draw parallels between games and management. The result of this mixture was Evolution Forge, which I will discuss in the last chapter of this book.

Clemens Lode
Author, *Kanban Remastered*
Düsseldorf, Germany, July 4th, 2017

Chapter 1

An Introduction...to StarCraft

There is a saying that if you want a successful software developer team, hire StarCraft players. Why? StarCraft not only trains you to react quickly, but it also teaches you valuable knowledge about management. For the players, this is not necessarily obvious, and management will often be viewed as something abstract and not related to their work. For an Agile coach, having a team with such background knowledge can help to speed up the learning process, and most importantly, increase the chances that the process will be accepted, becoming part of the team's culture.

For those unfamiliar with the game, let us first look at what StarCraft is. Then, in the following chapters, we will compare StarCraft with Kanban.

The computer game StarCraft puts you, the player, into a management position. Your task, in the beginning, is to manage three resources: minerals, Vespene gas, and supplies. The goal is to provide the "general" (also played by you) with military and support units. The specific management goal depends on the military scenario, but it usually revolves around defeating an enemy general.

Combat is based on a sophisticated version of a "rock, paper, and scissors" model (air, close-combat, and ranged units), so it is important to gather intelligence about what type of units the enemy produces. There are only a few effective ways of gathering intelligence, mainly moving a unit into the enemy's territory. The general decides on the strategy and provides the manager with the priorities based on the "market," the plan of your enemies: which units are most needed. The manager implements these priorities by using a specific build order, assigning worker units to produce factories, and factories to provide the military units or more worker units ("SCVs") in the "Command Center."

SCV · In StarCraft, the *SCV* is the all-purpose worker unit who gathers resources and constructs buildings. While it can defend itself, it is the weakest unit in the game. While it seems wise to produce new workers non-stop, you might want to temporarily sacrifice long-term growth with short-term gains: finding the right window of opportunity to build specific units, instead of investing into economic growth, might lead to you winning the game or at least getting ahead. Both in the game as in business, it does not matter how good your army or your product is, but how it is relative to your competition. Do not try to build a perfect army or perfect product. Check the market, check what consumers want: they want a better product than what the competitors are offering.

Command Center · In StarCraft, the *Command Center* is the first building you own. It can produce additional workers to mine resources. Building a second Command Center might speed up your worker production and resource gathering speed, but it is also costly. In a company, it could be compared with the basic structure of hiring new people, training, people management, etc. Both in StarCraft and in business, you are faced with the question of how many people you will hire for a project. Will you employ just a few and save money, or do you stop any other current investments and hire more people now to have them finish the project more quickly?

As in business, you will not win the game if you take forever to produce your "perfect product"—an army, in this case. Units produced as early as possible (or just at the right moment) can give you the upper hand in the game.

Beyond combat units, you also have carriers ("Dropships") and buildings. The former can be seen as a means of "deploying" units by transporting them to the battlefield. The latter can be used to block enemy units, or—wrongly-placed—to prevent your own movements, making deployment more difficult.

DROPSHIP · In StarCraft, the *Dropship* is basically a spaceship that can transport your units from one place to another. They can be seen as a means of "deploying" units. This element of the game is similar to what you have to do in a business. It is not enough to produce items, you also need to bring them to a place where your customers can see and buy them, be it a physical location or software on a web server. If appropriately coordinated, Dropships can be used for surprise attacks. Again, a concept you find in the business world: you need to plan your release of the product according to the external market forces, be it special dates (like Christmas) or competitor products. If you catch your competitor unprepared, the competitor might need time to adapt to your new product.

Resource management involves sending worker units to mineral fields and Vespene geysers in order to mine minerals and Vespene gas, which is used for production. These fields are depleted after a while, so you need to look out for and secure new locations that have resources. Also, you need to build supply depots to support your standing army. If you do not have enough supplies, your production stops, and you can no longer produce new units, so you have to plan for that in advance.

Besides minerals, gas, and supplies, time is another resource, as combat usually requires you to spend time micromanaging your units to move army groups and attack specific targets. As StarCraft is a real-time strategy game, any time used tending to combat cannot be used for managing to your production and resources. While you can queue movement commands at no cost, queuing production commands in your factories binds in advance resources that might be better used elsewhere (but allows for production without any interruption).

Even more complexity is added by the fact that there are three different factions, the option to research better weapons and armor, and tech-trees that are unlocked when constructing certain buildings. Last but not least, there are islands, cliffs, ramps, narrow pathways, and hills that add additional strategical and tactical challenges.

Now, this is all interesting in theory. But what does it look like? I recommend watching a few StarCraft games together (team building!) and discussing how elements of the game apply to the situation in your company. It is an excellent way of opening people up. By seeing it "in action," your team can more easily understand the management terms and concepts in Kanban. In fact, I encourage you to watch a few minutes of StarCraft replays right now or download the game (it's free) and play. If your manager asks, say that it is for research.

Done? Now on to the next chapter, comparing StarCraft to Kanban.

Chapter 2

Kanban and StarCraft

> When you choose to use Kanban as a method to drive change in your organization, you are subscribing to the view that it is better to optimize what already exists, because that is easier and faster and will meet with less resistance than running a managed, engineered, named-change initiative. Introducing a radical change is more complicated than incrementally improving an existing one.

—David J. Anderson, *Kanban: Successful Evolutionary Change for Your Technology Business*

In an organization, work can be distributed by two different approaches: "push" or "pull." You either get new work put on your desk and have to manage what to prioritize, or you ask for new tasks once you are finished with your old ones.

For example, "Gosplan," the agency responsible for central economic planning in the Soviet Union, used a push-based logistical system. At Gosplan, mathematical models predicted consumer behavior. Based on these models, the government created plans for the entire supply chain from the factory to the shops—with catastrophically bad results. For certain goods, there was always either too much or too little available. By contrast, "Kanban" is different:

> **KANBAN** · *Kanban* is Japanese and literally means "signboard." In the context of project management, the term is interpreted as "queue limitation." Kanban is a method designed to reduce unfinished work and wasteful inventory levels; it was originally developed at Toyota in the late 1940s. Back then, marketers at Toyota studied consumer behavior and supermarket stocking strategies and applied the ideas to logistics in industrial production. At Toyota, they had previously produced as much as possible, regardless of the demand from the market. In contrast, in supermarkets, customers take only what they need, expecting that the supermarket will be stocked up the next time they visit. The customer "pulls" an item from the shelves, and the supermarket makes sure to refill the shelves. This new Kanban method applied to production provided just as much as what was needed, just in time.

In addition to improving the production flow within a company, the significant advantage of Kanban is that it can be applied to the production phases of any existing organizational structure without having to change business processes. With the production flow being made transparent, you can detect where work piles up at one place and then introduce a limit of the amount of work that is in progress. As opposed to a "relay race" model where work is *pushed* to the next department and not followed through, in Kanban, work items are *pulled*, and work is stopped when the work limit of the following department hits its limit. This ensures that no work piles up or gets lost.

For example, cars need tires, a chassis, and a motor. Without a Kanban system, the three departments responsible for these parts will produce as much as possible: the company will always end up having either too many chassis, motors, or tires. If you instead have the departments check how many items are already in stock and stop producing when the stock is full, you save a lot of money. Sure, you might need these items later, but keeping a large inventory costs money that you could have invested elsewhere.

When presenting the situation in a business this way, it opens an objective discussion at the management level, ideally followed by incremental, evolutionary improvements. As opposed to Scrum which can be executed within a company "by name only," i.e., by following the ceremonies but never addressing core issues like multidisciplinary teams (see my book *Scrum Your Jira!*), Kanban is an organization-wide change management approach. Sure, Scrum involves creating lists of impediments, but it leaves it up to you how to deal with them.

> **SCRUM** · *Scrum* is a set of management tools that focuses a project back on the team level and uncovers internal and external impediments of the production process. By reducing communication paths through small, multidisciplinary teams, as well as frequent releases to the customer for review, the probability for project success can be improved even if the scope is not clear from the start. Also, work is divided into units of fixed lengths (sprints), which helps to plan future sprints with your team working at a sustainable speed.

Once Kanban is in place, the goal is to focus on the bottlenecks, and manage the flow. Discussions with management can best be lead by making things explicit. Identifying the bottlenecks themselves is just the start of your work. The real game-changer is to make explicit the current collaboration policies. This moves the discussion towards objectivity away from the abstract and maybe emotional or anecdotal arguments.

Usually, after an organization-wide introduction of Kanban, the first bottleneck is found at the top. If the organization is strongly hierarchical, work (decisions!) piles up at the desk of the organization's leader. In StarCraft, this is not much of a problem as playing in a team inherently includes decentralized control, but it helps to imagine how cumbersome a game would be if all decisions had to go over a third party's desk.

Even with a decentralized organization, a common argument against Kanban is that there will be idle time because one part of the organization might not be able to keep up with the rest. As a result, work piles up until it hits the limit. This is true, but the idea that you are doing a good job when everyone is working at 100 percent is not always accurate. This is comparable to, in StarCraft, trying to keep all building facilities active, whether you need the units at the moment or not—or maybe even refraining from building additional facilities fearing they would not be used all the time.

Ultimately, Kanban is about trying to improve the flow through an organization. It does not matter how many items you produce if your sales department cannot bring them to the customer. Likewise, in StarCraft, you must think about how you will use the units you produce, meaning how you will deploy them on the battlefield. Sure, creating as many units as possible is a viable strategy, just like you could throw your unsold products on the market at a lower price or keep them in storage "just in case" there is a sudden demand. But it is an inefficient strategy. *We can do better than mere local optimization.*

This rings especially true when looking at the market. While a company does not literally fight an enemy like you do in StarCraft, your competitors try to get your market share. Scouting your enemy and adjusting your strategy are central components in StarCraft, just as they are on the market. You need to have foresight and gain intelligence about them and maybe even think about making some risky investments before you are absolutely sure what others are doing. Why? Because waiting itself is a risk and you might miss the window of opportunity to be the first on the market with your product.

When all is in place, you can focus on communication. Using Kanban automatically leads to situations where a team is stuck insofar as it cannot pull new items to work on because the subsequent phases or departments have hit their work in progress limit. This encourages collaboration, where one team can help out the next and where teams sit together and think about how to prevent future bottlenecks. This element can be found in StarCraft, too, with very close team communication over audio during the game, as well as a review of the game and discussions about how to optimize team play afterward.

No matter the size or structure of your organization, take small steps. Kanban promotes this approach by starting with what you have in place and pointing out the bottlenecks. Where StarCraft falls short, by comparison, is the visualization of the "workflow." While tools eventually emerged that visualized some aspects of the replays, like your "actions per minute" symbolizing your workload, I know of no tool that does it the Kanban way and actually analyzes how much time you spend on each team or location and thus points out possible paths for optimization.

The closest software that does a similar job is Evolution Forge, which I will discuss in the last chapter of this book. It helps you to optimize your basic build order in small steps. Behind both approaches (Kanban and Evolution Forge) is the grand idea inherent in nature to leave things as they are and move forward without ever taking a step backward. Every change you make should improve the situation, and more substantial changes come into place as the sum of a whole number of smaller ones. In that regard, if you want to improve your StarCraft play the Kanban way, manual observation, maybe together with a critical friend, might be the best choice. On the other hand, if you want to learn the idea of Kanban with Star-Craft as an easy-to-understand reference, you have come to the right place!

Chapter 3

The General

> It is the sovereign's function to give broad instructions, but to decide on battle it is the function of the general.

—Sun Tsu, *The Art of War*

When implementing Agile methodology, some things are often overlooked: the organizational structure, the culture of the organization, and the people involved. Management looks at the market, hears "Agile" as the new buzzword, and thinks that this is the solution to the problems they (management) figure exist *within* the development department.

Introducing Agile is a change process, and change is hard. Why is it hard? Because over time, no matter how effectively an organization is structured, people fine-tune themselves to their organizational environment to at least have locally optimal work conditions. Changing any aspect of the organization then leads to those local optimizations becoming worthless, which leads to lower productivity and stronger resistance to change.

Because of this, when adopting Agile methods, an organization leader needs to take extra care to not only change one part, but also to change the whole organization (over time). Every part of the organization is involved because the idea of Agile is to combine different phases into one.

> **AGILE** · *Agile*, in the context of project management, is a method to reduce waste and delays by anticipating that plans will change. It is a set of methods which are most effective when applied to projects that are complex and chaotic, especially in product development. It also has its place in production, given that customer demand as well as productivity fluctuate.

> If words of command are not clear and distinct, if orders are not thoroughly understood, then the general is to blame. But, if orders are clear and the soldiers nevertheless disobey, then it is the fault of their officers.

—Sun Tsu, *The Art of War*

Kanban itself does not require specific roles within the team. What it does, though, is uncover problems in the organization that could be solved by assigning a single "product owner" to the team in order to give the team a vision and help with prioritizing tasks. Most often, the opposite is actually true; namely that you have *too many* product owners and overlapping responsibilities.

Imagine you have a software team and an architecture team, each with a separate supervising product owner. The software team needs machines for production deployment, but the product owner of the architecture team prioritized another project. In theory, in true Kanban fashion, the software team could move in to help out the architecture team and speed things up. In reality, this could fail for many reasons, such as lack of knowledge, access rights, or merely a difference of opinion about how the IT infrastructure should look. Also, the software team may get conflicting messages from both product owners about how to proceed. Focusing both development and IT architecture by putting them under the command of a single product owner can prevent these problems, and deployment could be streamlined.

Looking at StarCraft, you will encounter both scenarios in multi-player mode. There is no separate "general" role that oversees how a team should concentrate its forces. Instead, players individually decide where and how to attack. They are very opportunistic, quickly joining an attack by other members of the team with their available forces, and with little to no need for a manager at the top. Also, the most suitable (in terms of experience, size of force, proximity to the base, etc.) player automatically becomes a temporary leader in a specific situation.

In games like StarCraft, the general is in full control of land and air forces, from production to deployment. However, looking at military history, we see a totally different approach by some leaders. Sun Tsu, a Chinese general and military strategist in the "Spring and Autumn" period of Chinese history (722 BC to 470 BC), most famous for his work *The Art of War*, pointed out that it is essential for victory that generals are unconstrained by their superiors. A general must be free to wage war without interference. In World War II, the Allied command structure gave total authority to General Eisenhower, with four commanders representing the US Navy Group, United States Army Air Forces, US Army Group, and British Army Group. Each commander had clear responsibilities and was able to plan and execute operations independent of the other commanders. Land, air, and sea operations could be prepared by the individual commanders, and only joint operations that required a combination of groups had to involve Eisenhower directly.

One would expect an even better-organized hierarchy on the German side. However, there, you had a whole array of overlapping authorities with, for example, tank divisions being distributed among different army groups. The idea behind Hitler's organizational setup was primarily not about efficiency on the battlefield, but to retain control over the various factions within the German army and to have the final word on all decisions (i.e., to be the dictator). Before any of his commanders could execute an operation, it had to go over Hitler's desk because only he had all the necessary information required to make a strategic decision.

Imagine playing a game like StarCraft if team players had to share half their units with another player from the team—with the only possibility of talking to that player being via a third person who kept (informational) control this way. This allows the project to be micromanaged and controlled by a third person (basically a "dictator"); but you will lose the creativity and flexibility emerging from decentralized management.

In business, it is relatively easy to recognize the type of organization in which you are working. How are budgets allocated? Can individual departments work closely with other departments without the involvement of the CEO? Do the departments have the authority or can decisions be enforced only by mentioning the CEO (or adding him or her to the CC line in email messages)?

Sure, organizations ultimately have to remain unified. A CEO cannot have one department running wild. And there is usually a reason that an organization is the way it is, so merely changing the leadership style might actually result in even more chaos. Ultimately, it depends on the people involved. What type of people are they? Do they prefer a clean organizational chart with clear responsibilities, or can they operate only based on personal bonds and informational control? Do they share and work toward a shared vision, or do they prefer having a strong leader directing the way from case to case?

While every organization is different, you will find the latter type of organization more often in the field of sales-focused industries, while the former is usually to be found in production-focused industries. I think that both kinds of organizations have their place, but when you want to produce and run projects, you might want to think twice about wanting your organization to be controlled from the top.

What type of structure do you have in the organization where you work? Is it led by someone who is focused on production or on sales? How does that affect your experience with change in the organization?

Chapter 4

Idle Hands are the Manager's Workshop

StarCraft is a game of real-time strategy. Beginners who are new to this concept tend to make a critical mistake: building just one of each type of factory and filling its building queue. The significant advantage of this approach is that the factory works at 100 percent efficiency with no idle time, and you do not need to spend extra time issuing new commands to the factory. This is comparable to having specialists working on their pile of tasks with a 100 percent workload. From a classical project management view, this sounds perfect. No idle times and maximum productivity.

The problem is that having your factories run without idle times is not an objective of the game. You can pat yourself on the back for having such efficient factories, but you will not win the game because of it. In project management, these "factories" are your workers. A common management stance is, unfortunately, the idea that you have paid for the worker's time (40 hours a week) so you need to do something with him or her for 40 hours. But this is local optimization, more like an intellectual evasion, as in "I managed to occupy my workforce full-time, so I must be doing things right."

> **TIME-BOXING** · *Time-boxing* means to work on similar tasks during a specific time period. For example, instead of answering emails throughout the day, reserve half an hour each day to work through any unanswered emails. This eliminates the overhead of having to refocus between different tasks.

This approach of issuing commands requires management time. In StarCraft, you need to tend to combat and unit production at the same time. You need to interrupt managing your army and switch back and forth to and from production. The alternative is to plan in advance, spending or reserving additional resources, and risking being unable to react to changes. If you do not want to do that, you have to rely on time-boxing. Just as you focus on one task at any given moment in Kanban, you focus for a while on combat in StarCraft and only afterward switch back to managing production facilities.

Time-boxing with just a few workers or production facilities available can be expensive, though. One way to mitigate that in StarCraft is to invest in multiple production facilities. Your resources will otherwise pile up while you are not giving new production orders. You need only to switch back once, give all the orders, fill the production lines in your factories, and then return to combat with a fresh army waiting for you when you switch back the next time. While more facilities might ultimately mean that some of them will stay idle at times, you will be able to effectively turn over your resources into new units and replenish your forces more quickly compared to putting all your orders into a backlog pipeline which would bind resources you could use somewhere else: it takes time to plan and re-plan all those orders in the backlog when there are changes.

In Agile, you try to protect the team from having to go back and forth to their "production facilities" (e.g., new tasks from management, emails, interruptions in the room, bureaucracy) and instead work on a task until it is fully finished. In Kanban, with the limitation of simultaneous "in progress"-work, tasks do not get dragged along. There will be a stronger tendency to prevent tasks getting "90 percent" finished (with a business value of zero) and then left unfinished for a more pressing task. In this context, it might be interesting to mention the so-called "Pomodoro technique." It also uses time-boxing, although for the opposite reason: you should not work on a task for too long. Keep the tasks small by breaking them up into units and taking a break in between units. Looking at this with "Kanban eyes," this approach also helps to improve the flow of work. Individual tasks do not block the workflow for too long, and the next department can work on a task (or unit) sooner and in smaller increments.

> **POMODORO TECHNIQUE** · The *Pomodoro Technique* is a simple time management technique that allows focusing on one task, followed by a break, then moving on to the next task (Cirillo, *The Pomodoro Technique: The Acclaimed Time Management System That Has Transformed How We Work*).

Real emergencies require a slightly different approach. In Kanban, this is usually implemented by adding a horizontal "fast lane" with the highest priority and with a very low "work in progress" limit. For example, if the company website is down (or in StarCraft, if you face a sudden previously undetected attack), the task is pulled through the fast lane. The cost of not reacting significantly outweighs anything gained through time-boxing. The big question is what an emergency is, as opposed to a high-priority task. For example, do all customer requests require being put into the fast lane? What about requests from the CEO? The answers to these questions have to be documented and will constitute a "Service Level Agreement" (SLA). The involved parties have to understand that a requirement for immediate action comes at a cost. Sure, you could prioritize any CEO request as an emergency, but that also means that even the CEO's favorite project will suffer a delay. Even a buffer of a few hours where other tasks can be finished will help to smooth the otherwise disrupted workflow.

SERVICE LEVEL AGREEMENT · Thinking about Kanban leads to thinking about how different departments or teams work together. Written or not, there is always some sort of contract between the parties involved. A *Service Level Agreement* is such a contract and usually denotes the time between the initial request (e.g., for a software fix) until the first response by the team. This contract is established implicitly when people meet the first time or have the first telephone call. "Do you have a minute?" "Sure!" is a commonplace contract which translates into "Drop everything you are doing right now and focus on my problem." For the person requesting the service, this means that the supporting person is available on very short notice and ongoing work can be interrupted. In Kanban, with time-boxing, the answer is "Sure, but let me first finish what I am doing right now, and check if there is other, even more important work." If the current tasks are generally small, the request will still be worked on within a short time, but any overhead related to stopping and restarting ongoing tasks is prevented.

In StarCraft, an "SLA" would be anything that gives you more time to react by predicting your opponent's moves. Map scouting and detection help you to finish what you have started. Your SLAs will always be changing, though. If you have scouted your enemy preparing dropships to attack your base, you might want to set the reaction time very low. For some remote empty base, you might want to set the reaction time much higher or even ignore an attack altogether. Ultimately, the lesson is that it is OK to make small "mistakes" and to delay certain actions in favor of other, more important ones.

What about the other kind of problems, "defects"? Imagine you are attacking the enemy, moving your force near the enemy's base, only to discover that you are missing a central unit or ability. Maybe you forgot to build a scanner to detect invisible units, perhaps you are missing a medic, or perhaps you discover the upgrade your attack depended on is not finished. This is comparable to a situation in business when a story is supposedly finished but is found to be defective in the next phase (testing). What options do you have?

Imagining it again through the game of StarCraft, first, you could move your units all the way back to where they started, wait for the missing unit to be finished, then move back to a new attack. This certainly works but seems ineffective. A better way is to first check whether the attack can proceed anyway (i.e., if the product can be shipped anyway), or retreat to a safe position, and then (if still necessary) file a defect at the base to produce the additional unit or ask your teammate to help out. In business, the defective story will block the testing team, and they might hit their work-in-progress limit. If this occurs, they will either directly ask the development team to help out in typical Kanban fashion, or they will move the story to a parking position (not affecting the "work in progress" limit), adding a defect to the development team (affecting their "work in progress" limit).

WORK IN PROGRESS · The general idea in Agile project management is to limit the number of things you work on at the same time. In Scrum, you limit it by setting a fixed time frame (sprint) for a work package. In Kanban, you directly limit the number of tasks or projects worked on. This reduces overhead and automatically will lead to more complete tasks. If you can focus on but a few tasks and bring them to a finish, they are no longer dragged along half-finished without any value.

The solution you ultimately choose really depends on your business and the workflow. It might be unclear who actually caused the defect and who can fix it. Imagine the sales department is unable to close a deal; is it then a problem of the marketing department? Or is it the product itself that does not fit the customer's need? Implementing Kanban also means that you have to start asking those questions and thinking about a solution instead of relying on uncoordinated emails and case-by-case decisions. A good approach is to create a ticket but to assign it to a special support group who knows the product very well and have them analyze and decide which department most likely caused and/or can possibly fix it. And maybe the supposed defect is not a defect at all, so this would also shield other departments from false positives ("It's not a bug, it's a feature!").

Chapter 5

To the Frontlines

The central idea of Kanban is flow optimization. While Agile methods like Scrum are focused on creating and maintaining a central multidisciplinary team, Kanban accepts a non-optimal situation: teams are not 100 percent dedicated to a project, and project work is done in phases outside the core team. This is similar to the situation in StarCraft. There, you do not have a core team that executes building, movement, and combat. What you do have are multiple groups of units (or bases) and limited time to give orders. What do I mean by multiple groups? During the game, a StarCraft player has to switch between units and bases at different locations on the map, giving commands to solve current issues, like building new buildings or units, or attacking enemy units and building up a bridgehead.

Translating that into Kanban requires some thought. Imagine that every StarCraft group gets new "tasks" whenever something should be done, strategically or tactically. When you produce a new unit, then that unit needs to be deployed to a location; when you see an enemy dropship flying by, then your units need to intercept it; when you complete the construction of a new base, you need to start gathering resources, etc. Likewise, the amount of time you invest at each group location to work through those tasks relates to the manpower you would have in a Kanban project. You can imagine that it is not wise to spend minutes working on your economy while your base is overrun. Likewise, if you do nothing but defend your base and micromanage your units, work (like expanding the economy) piles up at other locations. A good StarCraft player will be able to analyze the situation and surmise that maybe she spent too time in one location while ignoring the tasks piling up at another. So, she will correct the workflow to devote more time to other tasks as well, helping out those groups.

With time being an essential resource in StarCraft, novice players are inclined to spend as little time as possible on their actions. They may place buildings wherever there is space at that moment and then move on to the next army group to do the same. Units then might have to maneuver around these misplaced buildings. Or, perhaps factories are placed far from the front line: precious seconds as forces will take longer to replenish or mount an attack. Searching for individual misplaced buildings in order to give new production commands can slow forces down.

> **TECH-DEBT** · In software terms, "tech debt" usually refers to code that later needs to be rewritten or systems that later have to be scrapped and rebuilt and reconfigured. The term can apply to anything that saves you time now but has to be paid back later in the form of additional work.

More advanced StarCraft players seldom to never take up such "tech debt." They do not place buildings in the walking path of the units. They concentrate production facilities so that when they quickly switch back to them during combat, they save those precious seconds that could give them the edge in micromanaging combat. Their game flow is highly optimized; they do not spend too much time in one place. What can we learn from their approach?

Of course, I do not want to imply that you should *never* take up debt. Remember that you do not want to build a perfect product but instead to strike at the right time with the right product. Cutting corners in that regard can be OK when connecting it to a clear purpose and when keeping in mind the added later costs. Where Kanban can help is identifying when fast-tracking a task can be useful, and setting up reminders to work on it by adding it to the Kanban board. Once the objective is achieved, this task should be worked on soon because it will continue to add costs to the deployment of your existing units (or your product) or the time needed to produce new units (or products). Keep in mind, though, to limit the number of tech debt tasks and to *eventually* work on them. If the tech debt reaches the final product, you might have been better off changing your idea of when a task is "done" instead of aiming for higher quality but never living up to it.

In terms of reporting development speed, you might want to *not* (or only partly) include any fast-tracked tasks, as they ultimately do not add to the finished product. Toward the "general" (business), it is essential to visibly demonstrate that a decision to speed up a project at the cost of such tech debt has consequences. There needs to be a justification for how this early time-saving ultimately saves —not costs—money.

How does Kanban solve the problem of long waiting times?

Another point is how to actually deploy your units to the far-away front lines. StarCraft provides an automatic feature where you can just set a waypoint for each building, and the units will then, one by one, move toward that point. The big problem here is that this can cause additional costs. First, those units in transit are hard to control as they are individual groups spread over half of the map. Second, your supply line of new units can easily be disrupted by an enemy's strike-force. Both of these problems also appear in regular production within a business. Some of the tasks might require long regulatory processes or are interrupted by long delays for ordering new hardware prototypes or even disrupted by supplier problems or competitors. Inside the company itself, handing over a lot of small tasks one-by-one to the next team might likewise interrupt their work as they might need briefing for each item.

Hand over reasonably sized tasks to the next department. This is the equivalent of sending out groups of units over the battlefield instead of trying to micromanage individual units. Kanban mitigates problems with external suppliers by at least optimizing the throughput and workflow so that the cost, up until ordering a new prototype or starting the regulatory process, is lower. Also, consider starting the same lengthy process multiple times and earlier. Imagine you are building a new mainboard for your machine and the supplier will take 10 weeks to finish it. Instead of working for four weeks, finalizing the board and sending out the order, send out the first order after two weeks with a half-finished board, then send out another order after four. Sure, you will still get the final board only after 14 weeks, but maybe you will discover a problem with the first prototype after 12 weeks. You will have reduced the delay for a possible defect by two weeks at additional costs for ordering. In some cases, if your development time, not your ordering expenses, is the bottleneck, this might be worthwhile. Translated into StarCraft, it simply means that you can send out the second army group while the first is still on its way. Maybe the first army group will defeat the enemy. If it has to retreat, your second army group is ready to support them —lower risk at a higher cost.

Another Kanban approach is to include the external supplier as a part of your supply chain: the visualization on your Kanban board will show them to be the bottleneck, with work piling up on their side. Ask yourself how you can help them! Maybe they can produce a first prototype with more lax specifications; possibly provide them only with test cases and acceptance criteria instead of asking them to build it precisely to your specifications. Perhaps have your team visit their factory to speed up the setup, or invite them to your meetings to get them started right away once you are ready. In software development, make use of mock systems or models that simulate the systems you ultimately want to connect to or users who will use your system. Find people within your company to test unfinished prototypes that have not yet passed the long internal regulatory processes. Early feedback is the key. In StarCraft, you could think about building production facilities right near the front line (they are relatively cheap!), or you could spend some time re-examining your current building setup. Do not be shy about destroying buildings in your way or building extra facilities closer to the front line to speed up the deployment.

In the end, though, you need to have an idea about how to release your product. Start with delineating your release process. Writing everything down helps to make clear which parts of the release process are unfinished. All too often, a company produces something without really knowing how to distribute, market, or sell the item—this is mostly true for companies who have faced little to no competition, be it because they are the only one on the market or because they are a startup.

Likewise, in StarCraft, ask yourself what you will do with a unit. Is a dropship ready to be deployed? Do you have set waypoints? What army group will you assign it to? What is its purpose? The time a unit just stands there unused costs as much as the value another unit would produce during that time.

Ultimately, all the points mentioned above are pretty obvious *once you see them.* The key is to visualize what is actually going on. Far too often, I have noticed that features are produced but then never used. This is partly because of the 100 percent fallacy mentioned previously, which leads to a lot of items getting "pushed" to the next department as opposed to being "pulled" by, ultimately, the customer.

One good exercise in StarCraft is to make a cooperative play where one player solely commands combat units while the other player solely commands production units and facilities. Observe how they develop a strategy of communication. Will they favor "push" or "pull"?

Chapter 6

Scouting the Market

One significant element of the game StarCraft is using is a "fog of war." As opposed to games like chess, where the whole situation is visible, and you can act strategically, in StarCraft, you have to constantly visit the enemy's bases to check what they are doing. Only with constant feedback can you adapt your own strategy to be ready when they try to attack you. You need to have the right force, at the right time and place, to counter your enemy. In business, it is the same. It may be with the difference that you have a lot more time to "scout" your competitors, but it is often much harder to get reliable information.

Given that your competitor also scouts you, this results in an interesting dynamic. Depending on how fast and competitive the industry you are working in is and how reliably information can be gathered, this can require different approaches. Often, over time, the most flexible and adaptive product wins. If you can change strategies quickly, you have an easier time countering your enemy's change of strategy (or adapting more quickly to a changing demand from the market). Kanban can help when those changes are coming from the demand side pulling through the company, or by small changes (e.g., turnover) within the company, which are also manageable by the Kanban workflow.

In terms of investment in market research, you might want to wait until you have scouted the enemy before you decide what type of units you will build. This way, you keep the risk to a minimum. On the other hand, when you have scouted the enemy and have the information, it might be too late to react. You might have some sort of product life cycle management (PLM) in place to first determine the feasibility of the product. This is sometimes easy to do when all you have to manage is resources. Sometimes, though, you are wandering in the unknown and only by implementing your plan will it show if it is feasible or not; an example would be engineering (cars, scientific instruments, rockets, etc.). Now, this is similar to scouting. While you can undoubtedly make projections that the enemy will not attack you with a battle cruiser within the first few minutes because you know precisely with what resources they have started, you do not know their exact strategy.

Ultimately, you have to make a balancing choice. If risk is what you want to minimize, wait with any decision or investment until you have the information you need and know what is feasible. Your product will be on the market later, but you will save any initial investment you might have lost if it turns out it is not feasible. But keep in mind that risk stems not just from feasibility, but also from the marketplace. If you miss the window of opportunity to sell your product, you will have spent a lot more money and get no return.

The best approach is to divide your product into modules whose feasibility can be determined independently. Once the feasibility of one module is established, you can start with its implementation while you are still determining the feasibility of the next. You would already have begun building your resource gatherers, supply depots, and basic technological buildings even though you have not established the feasibility of your strategy. It is a risk, but a lower risk than if you waited.

Chapter 7

Team Communication

> Developing an increased level of trust with other teams can enable the harder things.

—David J. Anderson, *Kanban: Successful Evolutionary Change for Your Technology Business*

In StarCraft, as in any organization, a significant danger in terms of teamwork is when people draw circles around their field of expertise and stop feeling responsible for the world outside. Statements like "it's my game, if you are getting overrun by the enemy, that's your problem" sum up a prevailing attitude among amateur team players. When the teammate is in trouble, instead of using the opportunity to either help to defend against or attack the enemy, new players tend to blame their partner.

In Scrum, this problem is approached by making the core team into a multidisciplinary team which is able to deliver the complete product or feature without having to coordinate every step with other departments. Its members work on all tasks, as opposed to being nothing but specialists in their respective fields of expertise. There might still be outside specialists providing expertise in a support function, but they are not actually working on project tasks. There still is a bubble, but it is set up in a smart way.

In StarCraft, a comparable element to specialization can be found in the early part of the game, when one player decides to follow a single-minded build order to rush the enemy with an advanced type of unit instead of also building basic units to help the teammate against an early attack. Yes, you might be faster by focusing on just your own base, but ultimately, you will sacrifice the advantage of joint team operations. These kinds of strategies are called "cheezy" for a reason: they have a good chance of working if you are lucky, but in general, if your teammate does not protect your back and can fend for himself, you might lose.

In Kanban, the "bubbles" around the Kanban teams are being removed. When the work in one project phase is piling up, either this can serve as a signal for upper management to fix the bottleneck, or the one team simply helps the other until the number of "work in progress" items is again below the limit. This is nothing different than helping out your teammate in StarCraft during an attack.

Now, how do you interact with your Agile team? In StarCraft, the best team knows how it thinks; it knows how every team member acts and reacts without having to check. The basic principles of Agile ring true here as well: personal contact is better than abstract communication. The most effective teams have moved from sharing text messages to voice chat. And they have not done it because text messages would not convey the necessary information. Voice chat simply offers a means of constant communication and synchronization. It reduces the possibility for errors when you describe what you do and also re-focuses the team constantly on the objectives instead of getting lost in details and micromanagement—a common novice mistake.

The downside of voice as well as text chat is the immediacy, which can also be distracting. In your Agile teams, make sure to monitor ongoing discussions to prevent them from escalating, and log and reduce external distractions by channeling them in one place (e.g., a central email address for all questions to the team) or focusing them in regular meetings.

Beyond mere information exchange, a critical factor of good teams is trust. If they do not know each other, people on a team will have trouble knowing whether the other team members will come to the rescue. Working with teams, my recommendation is to make sure that they can build a healthy, trusting relationship with each other. One symptom of unhealthy team relationships is when one of the team members plays the "hero," thinking the team or project needs to be saved. Here, Kanban can help by predicting the workload of individual team members and explaining how a "hero" will eventually become a bottleneck.

As with teams in StarCraft, teams in your business also have to "play" together. It takes a while until a team has formed, and formed teams usually consist of compatible personality types who know each other's strengths and weaknesses. Be aware when, due to some management decisions, teams are broken off: new teams will have to invest a significant amount of time in forming themselves.

Finally, StarCraft and Kanban have the most important thing in common: respect. While you can find mean and self-centered people everywhere, in StarCraft, there is (or was) a particular culture of respect. Common courtesy is to wish your opponent good luck at the start of the game, and tell him that it was a good game at the end— instead of hurling insults against him. Respect is also a pillar of Kanban. Of course, you respect your team, but you should also respect all the project stakeholders instead of plotting or scheming against some of them. This does not necessarily mean agreeing with everyone, but at least hearing them out and trying to take their views objectively. And treating them like human beings. When you leave a project, thank the stakeholders for their trust in you and for the work you both managed to do together. Likewise, if someone from your team leaves, thank them for their work rather than complaining about people leaving the team.

Who are the stakeholders in StarCraft? Well, obviously the enemies! Sure, you could build your great base and gather all the resources from the map, but where is the fun in playing alone? Your enemy helps you to become a better player. Your enemy helps you to shape the actual product you are both working on: an exciting game to play and watch. That is the reason you both started the game. Your enemy stands symbolically for the "market demand," just like (some) stakeholders can represent the market. Show them respect. Build trust between each other in order to enjoy the game together.

Chapter 8

Evolutionary
Improvements

An single match of StarCraft could be compared to a single iteration of a new product, a single evolutionary step after which you can examine the replay and discuss and improve your strategy and tactics.

This is time-consuming, so to help this process, I have developed a tool, Evolution Forge, that speeds up these learning iterations. It works by running an abstract simulation of StarCraft to test how a particular strategy would actually play out. So, instead of having to play game after game yourself, you can use the tool to quickly try out different strategies and see how fast you would be in the real game.

On top of just testing the speed of a strategy, this tool was designed to come up with new random strategies to reach a predefined goal (e.g., building 10 Space Marines in the Barracks) as quickly as possible. I programmed it to make random changes to a basic strategy, run the simulation, test its speed, and repeat the process until the program came up with a faster strategy. Then the program used that faster strategy, made random changes to it, and on and on. In small steps, the strategy became more and more efficient at reaching the goal.

> **SPACE MARINE** · The *Space Marine* is the basic combat unit in StarCraft. It is the dominant unit in the early part of the game, the only protection between your own base and the enemy. Space Marines are produced in the Barracks and will be used as a basic example, in this book, for build orders. Just like a product needs several parts to be able to make a single sale, a lone Space Marine is the weakest unit of the game. Their real power shows when they act in a group, with other units supporting them.

> **BARRACKS** · In StarCraft, the *Barracks* are the first production facility to produce combat units (the Space Marines). Building the Barracks also allows building other, more technologically advanced, production and research facilities, making the Barracks

> a cornerstone of any build order. The Barracks can be compared
> with the very basic structure of an enterprise with sales and mar-
> keting: No matter how good your product is, you still need to
> market and sell it!

Unfortunately, the program regularly got stuck because, most of the
time, randomly rearranging your strategy leads to the exact same
(or worse) outcome (in this case, time until the set of goal units were
produced). To really improve, more substantial changes would have
been necessary. But larger (random) changes typically lead to worse
results. Does this sound familiar? It is the same situation that can
be found in companies where large process changes are introduced.
Suddenly, the promised improvement turns out to slow down rather
than speed up project work! What to do?

In nature, transitory states become apparent in hindsight. Only then
does it become clear how one thing led to the next. At no time could
you point to one gene that could dramatically change a life form. No
single change is a significant improvement over another because all
the parts of a life form are highly optimized. Changing one thing
might hinder the optimization of another. So, at first glance, it is a
mysterious wonder how natural processes led up to the creation of
complex organs. Looking more closely at the evolutionary process,
it becomes clear that evolution really is based on minimal changes.
Nature cannot take a break for a few generations, working on a new
prototype. Every single change has to make the life form more fit
to its environment.

> To suppose that the eye with all its inimitable contrivances
> for adjusting the focus to different distances, for admitting
> different amounts of light, and for the correction of spherical
> and chromatic aberration, could have been formed by natu-
> ral selection, seems, I freely confess, absurd in the highest de-
> gree. Yet reason tells me, that if numerous gradations from
> a perfect and complex eye to one very imperfect and simple,

each grade being useful to its possessor, can be shown to exist; if further, the eye does vary ever so slightly, and the variations be inherited, which is certainly the case; and if any variation or modification in the organ be ever useful to an animal under changing conditions of life, then the difficulty of believing that a perfect and complex eye could be formed by natural selection, though insuperable by our imagination, can hardly be considered real.

—Charles Darwin, *The Origin of Species*

On its own, a *part* of an eye cannot see; it would be the same as if you (in business) involved only a single department in product creation. A product without marketing or sales literally will not sell, just like you cannot sell or market if you have no product, just like a part of an eye cannot see.

Or can it? Part of an eye *can* see if that "part" refers to an earlier stage in its evolutionary development. Just as you can release a software product before it has all its features, you can build a simpler version of an eye that *can* see. What is the basic element of an eye? The cells that react to incoming light. Imagine you have just a *plane* of cells that react to light. What can they "see"? They cannot detect the direction from which the light comes, so all they can perceive is whether their environment is light or dark.

You might say, well, this is not an eye! An eye sees images! But a shade of gray is an image, just an image of very low quality. And that is the core idea: find an indicator that describes your product that can easily scale. For an eye, it would be the resolution and definition of the perceived image. For example, if your project is about building a car, maybe make the indicator speed in combination with fuel usage per 100 miles. If you write a book, try to split it into independent chapters. You can then write one chapter, add the front and back matter and a basic cover, and you have your first version. It might be short, and it might not be finished in terms of editing, but it is a book! Then add one chapter after the other, bringing it to a finish resulting in a complete book.

Coming back to our eye, we could bend the plane of cells in our next version. This allows a very rough orientation about where the light is coming from. We could bend it further and further until we have a basic pinhole camera with a small entrance for the light and a circular layer of cells that can detect the light. Later, we could add a lens and gradually improve the vision until we have an eye comparable to ours.

Complicated things can be built by finding a *ramp* which we can use to gradually make the things better. Once you discover that ramp for your product or organization, improvement becomes very easy. And Kanban can help you find that ramp without making substantial changes to the organization. Kanban itself is a passive process on top of your existing processes. It only shows you where you should go. You can then take that path in small steps without ever disrupting your organization.

For my software tool, Evolution Forge, my solution was to find such a ramp. Instead of focusing on just one thing, namely the time until the goal is reached, I looked at the overall quality of a strategy. In StarCraft, I simply included the amount of mined resources as an indicator to compare two strategies with the same goal time. When a strategy achieves the same set of goal units with more resources in the bank, it gets ranked higher and is selected for the next generation in the evolutionary process. This is similar to comparing two project plans with the same release date but different costs.

I also apply this principle of small changes in my personal life. I follow the idea of removing one thing each day. I ask myself: do I really need that? How do I benefit from a particular item? Does the happiness it brings outweigh its upkeep? It is one way of simplifying my life. It might not pay off immediately, but eventually, it might just be what gets me ahead, having a clean workspace and being able to focus on what is essential. This helps me to get unstuck, it gives me a "ramp" to improve when I do not see the next step. Likewise, when working as an Agile coach, when there is some idle time between tasks, I check the (real or virtual) project room to see if there is one thing that could be cleaned up or removed. When you employ this approach, step by step, your workspace becomes better, and people see steady progress—the core principle for motivation.

Kanban is usually focused on the flow of work and resources through a company. What is often missed is to also improve the *processes* of the individual workers or the workspaces themselves. This can require some outside encouragement to change inefficient processes that have become ingrained in an individual's work habits. It sometimes requires throwing things away, ending unproductive projects, and maybe even firing people who might actually be much happier in another job. Think about scrapping 10 percent of your current projects and processes every year. If you do not, you will eventually end up with a company that is just busy with itself. Cutting away the unnecessary stuff makes room to focus on what is actually essential—that applies to businesses with complex and opaque organizational problems as it does to life in general.

Instead of trying to implement massive organizational programs, think about what small things you can change to improve the situation. While minor changes lead only to minor improvements, at least they can be easily implemented, and their improvements are easy to track. For example, saving your team a few minutes each day by having pens and paper ready when the meetings start might not turn around a failed project or double the sales. But it is something you can be sure will improve team performance. So, instead of thinking about the grand plan and huge change processes, think about what you can improve *now*. These small improvements might eventually pave the way for more substantial after all.

Teach your employees the costs of not cleaning up—program code, their workspaces, or projects that just increase costs and bring no value. Instead of rushing in to try to keep your team busy with project tasks when they are finished with their current tasks, have them work on issues that they want to fix. Ask the people who are actually working on the project what could be improved: even fixing small things adds up and will give your company the energy to address more complicated problems. Ultimately, teach your teams to tackle the lesser issues when they are stuck on a larger problem.

Likewise, teach management and product owners not to take up any "monkeys"—work that should be done by someone else, not by them. Advise them that instead of trying to be the hero, adding more and more meetings to their schedules, they could do one or two projects and be fully focused.

Learning from nature requires us to unlearn the hubris of thinking that big drastic changes are needed for positive outcomes. The bigger the ideas of how to change a company, the more in peril that company probably is. People promising big dreams bet on circumstance that luck will somehow turn into their favor, grandstanding as the hero. But they will likely have left the scene when it comes to implementing those ideas or will blame others or the very circumstance they bet on if their plan fails.

There is a time to stand up as a hero, though. Standing up against big, "revolutionary" ideas that will supposedly turn everything around and focusing on what can be done incrementally now: that is the time to show courage and perseverance.

Other Books (available in paperback and e-book!)

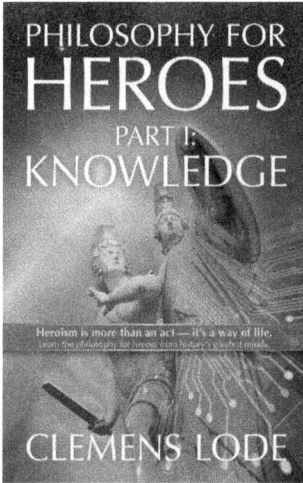

PHILOSOPHY FOR HEROES
PART I:
KNOWLEDGE
Heroism is more than an act — it's a way of life.
Learn the philosophy for heroes from history's greatest minds.
CLEMENS LODE

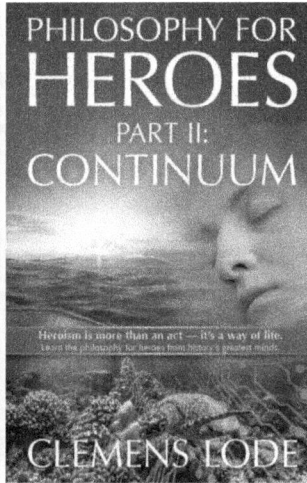

PHILOSOPHY FOR HEROES
PART II:
CONTINUUM
Heroism is more than an act — it's a way of life.
Learn the philosophy for heroes from history's greatest minds.
CLEMENS LODE

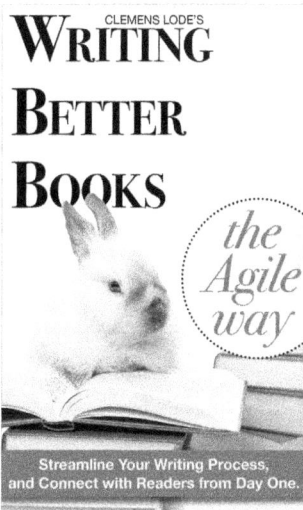

CLEMENS LODE'S
WRITING
BETTER
BOOKS
the Agile way
Streamline Your Writing Process,
and Connect with Readers from Day One.

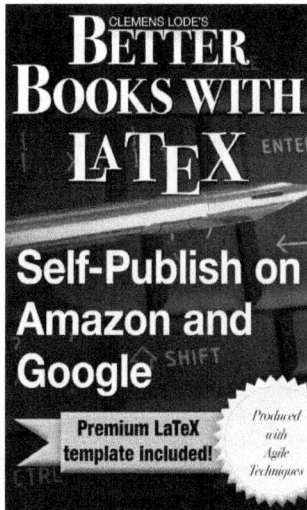

CLEMENS LODE'S
BETTER
BOOKS WITH
LaTeX
Self-Publish on
Amazon and
Google
Premium LaTeX template included!
Produced with Agile Techniques

The Author

Clemens Lode works as an author as well as a coach for software teams throughout Europe. He lives in Düsseldorf (Germany). You can follow him on Facebook (https://fb.me/ClemensLode) or Twitter (https://www.twitter.com/ClemensLode), or just drop him a line (clemens@lode.de).

❝ What I cannot create, I do not understand.

—Richard Feynman

Glossary

A

Agile • *Agile*, in the context of project management, is a method to reduce waste and delays by anticipating that plans will change. It is a set of methods which are most effective when applied to projects that are complex and chaotic, especially in product development. It also has its place in production, given that customer demand as well as productivity fluctuate.

B

Barracks • In StarCraft, the *Barracks* are the first production facility to produce combat units (the Space Marines). Building the Barracks also allows building other, more technologically advanced, production and research facilities, making the Barracks a cornerstone of any build order. The Barracks can be compared with the very basic structure of an enterprise with sales and marketing: No matter how good your product is, you still need to market and sell it!

C

Command Center • In StarCraft, the *Command Center* is the first building you own. It can produce additional workers to mine resources. Building a second Command Center might speed up your worker production and resource gathering speed, but it is also costly. In a company, it could be compared with the basic structure of hiring new people, training, people management, etc. Both in StarCraft and in business, you are faced with the question of how many people you will hire for a project. Will you employ just a few and save money, or do you stop any other current investments and hire more people now to have them finish the project more quickly?

D

Dropship • In StarCraft, the *Dropship* is basically a spaceship that can transport your units from one place to another. They can be seen as a means of "deploying" units. This element of the game is similar to what you have to do in a business. It is not enough to produce items, you also need to bring them to a place where your customers can see and buy them, be it a physical location or software on a web server. If appropriately coordinated, Dropships can be used for surprise attacks. Again, a concept you find in the business world: you need to plan your release of the product according to the external market forces, be it special dates (like Christmas) or competitor products. If you catch your competitor unprepared, the competitor might need time to adapt to your new product.

K

Kanban • *Kanban* is Japanese and literally means "signboard." In the context of project management, the term is interpreted as "queue limitation." Kanban is a method designed to reduce unfinished work and wasteful inventory levels; it was originally developed at Toyota in the late 1940s. Back then, marketers at Toyota studied consumer behavior and supermarket stocking strategies and applied the ideas to logistics in industrial production. At Toyota, they had previously produced as much as possible, regardless of the demand from the market. In contrast, in supermarkets, customers take only what they need, expecting that the supermarket will be stocked up the next time they visit. The customer "pulls" an item from the shelves, and the supermarket makes sure to refill the shelves. This new Kanban method applied to production provided just as much as what was needed, just in time.

P

Pomodoro Technique • The *Pomodoro Technique* is a simple time management technique that allows focusing on one task, followed by a break, then moving on to the next task (Cirillo, *The Pomodoro Technique: The Acclaimed Time Management System That Has Transformed How We Work*).

S

Scrum • *Scrum* is a set of management tools that focuses a project back on the team level and uncovers internal and external impediments of the production process. By reducing communication paths through small, multidisciplinary teams, as well as frequent releases to the customer for review, the probability for project success can be improved even if the scope is not clear from the start. Also, work is divided into units of fixed lengths (sprints), which helps to plan future sprints with your team working at a sustainable speed.

SCV • In StarCraft, the *SCV* is the all-purpose worker unit who gathers resources and constructs buildings. While it can defend itself, it is the weakest unit in the game. While it seems wise to produce new workers non-stop, you might want to temporarily sacrifice long-term growth with short-term gains: finding the right window of opportunity to build specific units, instead of investing into economic growth, might lead to you winning the game or at least getting ahead. Both in the game as in business, it does not matter how good your army or your product is, but how it is relative to your competition. Do not try to build a perfect army or perfect product. Check the market, check what consumers want: they want a better product than what the competitors are offering.

Service Level Agreement • Thinking about Kanban leads to thinking about how different departments or teams work together. Written or not, there is always some sort of contract between the parties involved. A *Service Level Agreement* is such a contract and usually denotes the time between the initial request (e.g., for a software fix) until the first response by the team. This contract is established implicitly when people meet the first time or have the first telephone call. "Do you have a minute?" "Sure!" is a commonplace contract which translates into

"Drop everything you are doing right now and focus on my problem." For the person requesting the service, this means that the supporting person is available on very short notice and ongoing work can be interrupted. In Kanban, with time-boxing, the answer is "Sure, but let me first finish what I am doing right now, and check if there is other, even more important work." If the current tasks are generally small, the request will still be worked on within a short time, but any overhead related to stopping and restarting ongoing tasks is prevented.

Space Marine • The *Space Marine* is the basic combat unit in StarCraft. It is the dominant unit in the early part of the game, the only protection between your own base and the enemy. Space Marines are produced in the Barracks and will be used as a basic example, in this book, for build orders. Just like a product needs several parts to be able to make a single sale, a lone Space Marine is the weakest unit of the game. Their real power shows when they act in a group, with other units supporting them.

S

Tech-Debt • In software terms, "tech debt" usually refers to code that later needs to be rewritten or systems that later have to be scrapped and rebuilt and reconfigured. The term can apply to anything that saves you time now but has to be paid back later in the form of additional work.

Time-boxing • *Time-boxing* means to work on similar tasks during a specific time period. For example, instead of answering emails throughout the day, reserve half an hour each day to work through any unanswered emails. This eliminates the overhead of having to refocus between different tasks.

W

Waterfall • *Waterfall* is a project management method where a product moves through a number of phases before a final version is finished for release. Compared to Agile, the problem with this method is that it requires additional communication channels between the individual phases and the time until a team or company gets feedback from a customer is generally much longer with Waterfall than Agile.

Work In Progress • The general idea in Agile project management is to limit the number of things you work on at the same time. In Scrum, you limit it by setting a fixed time frame (sprint) for a work package. In Kanban, you directly limit the number of tasks or projects worked on. This reduces overhead and automatically will lead to more complete tasks. If you can focus on but a few tasks and bring them to a finish, they are no longer dragged along half-finished without any value.

Bibliography

Cirillo, Francesco. *The Pomodoro Technique: The Acclaimed Time Management System That Has Transformed How We Work*. Crown Business, 2017. ISBN: 978-1524760700.

Lode, Clemens. *Kanban Remastered*. Clemens Lode Verlag e.K., 2017. ISBN: 978-3-945586-68-6.

—   *Scrum Your Jira!* Clemens Lode Verlag e.K., 2017. ISBN: 978-3-945586-69-3.

Index

Note that the indexes that resemble a file structure (e.g., /back/amazon.tex) refer to a paragraph in the book where the contents of the file from the Overleaf template are discussed.

An Important Final Note

Writers are not performance artists. While there are book signings and public readings, most writers (and readers) follow their passion alone in their writing spaces at home, in a café, in a library, at the beach, or at a mountain retreat.

*What applause is for the musician, **reviews** are for the writer.*

Books create a community among readers; you can share your thoughts among all those who will or have read this book.

Please leave a thoughtful, honest review and help me to create such a community on the platform on which you have acquired this book. What did you like, what can be improved? To whom would you recommend it?

Thank you, also in the name of all the other readers who will be better able to decide whether this book is right for them. A positive review will increase the reach of the book; a negative review will improve the quality of the next book. I welcome both!

thank you

> Two things destroy businesses—mediocrity and making it about yourself.

—Halt and Catch Fire